"Shelley is a heroine who has returned from a difficult life journey with news of healing. Her account will aid anyone seeking personal growth, more fulfilling relationships, and transformation—and who isn't?"

LARRY DOSSEY, MD
AUTHOR, *HEALING WORDS: THE POWER OF PRAYER AND THE PRACTICE OF MEDICINE*

"Full of spiritual insights, practical wisdom, and clinical understanding, *The Sampler* will help you see yourself with new eyes and challenge you to move from victim to victor and become the healthy, free person you were created to be. Shelley's ten life-enhancing concepts are truly empowering and life-affirming."

NANCY STAFFORD
ACTRESS AND AUTHOR OF *BEAUTY BY THE BOOK: SEEING YOURSELF AS GOD SEES YOU*

"With great generosity and courage, Shelley reveals the difficult life lessons she has learned. Despite her many physical and emotional scars, Shelley not only relishes what God has done in her life, but also uses her experiences to help and encourage others. *The Sampler* will encourage everybody caught in the pain of the past that God can do great things in their lives."

BARBARA M. HOUSTON, PSYD
ASSOCIATE PROFESSOR, HIGH DESERT CHRISTIAN COLLEGE, BEND, OREGON

"Shelley Maurice-Maier has written simply but elegantly and honestly about universal issues of life: discouragement, serious illness, betrayal, unmet expectations, and more. Her evaluation of responses to human frailties is honest and heartening. Most encouraging is her affirmation that a relationship with God is both essential and indispensable in meeting the challenges of our own individual journeys. I happily recommend *The Sampler* to anyone seeking to live with integrity."

CAROL ABRAHAM
EXECUTIVE ASSISTANT,
NORTHWEST PROFESSIONAL MANAGEMENT

"This is the compelling story of one person's journey to discover the keys to living a happy and fulfilling life. Shelley's discoveries are presented in a way that is easy to understand and remember. This little book is a must read for those of us on a similar quest."

DONALD G. STEWART, PHD
PASTORAL COUNSELOR, WESTSIDE CHURCH,
BEND, OREGON

"It's one thing to expound precepts that are healing and close to the reality of all things—but quite another to be an exemplar of those truths. Shelley's personal challenges carry a ring of authenticity. 'I was there,' the book says."

WILLIAM LUCE
BROADWAY PLAYWRIGHT

The
SAMPLER

10 Life-Enhancing Concepts
Right At Your Fingertips

SHELLEY
MAURICE-MAIER

ABIDING BOOKS

THE SAMPLER
published by Abiding Books

© 2004 by Shelley Maurice-Maier
International Standard Book Number: 0-9744284-1-8

Cover photo and design by Stephen Gardner
Interior design by Pamela McGrew

Unless otherwise indicated, Scripture quotations are from:
The Holy Bible, New International Version © 1973, 1984 by International Bible Society,
used by permission of Zondervan Publishing House
Other Scripture quotations:
The Holy Bible, New King James Version (NKJV) © 1984 by Thomas Nelson, Inc.

Printed in the United States of America

For information:
ABIDING BOOKS • P. O. BOX 243 • CONDON, OREGON 97823
www.abidingbooks.com

Library of Congress Cataloging-in-Publication Data

Maier, Shelley Maurice.
  The sampler : ten life-enhancing concepts right at your fingertips / by
Shelley Maurice Maier.— 2nd ed.
     p. cm.
  ISBN 0-9744284-1-8 (hardcover : alk. paper)
  1. Christian life. I. Title.

  BV4501.3.M245 2004
  248.4—dc22

                              2004003465

    04 05 06 07 08 09—10 9 8 7 6 5 4 3 2 1 0

To my beloved mother, Mickey
I knew that you knew…
but my message to you on your
fortieth birthday still holds true:

Dear Mom,
If in my life I become just half the woman you are,
I will know I have done well as your daughter.
I love you.
Shelley

Contents

Unable are the Loved to die
For Love is Immortality,
Nay, it is Deity—
Unable they that Love—to die
For Love transforms Vitality into Divinity.

—EMILY DICKINSON

The Sampler

When I was young, I very much wanted to please my mother. I was always asking her, "Mama, will you be proud of me if I become a librarian?" "Mama, will you be proud of me if I become a cowgirl?"

She would always answer, "Yes, I will always be proud of you, honey."

When I reached my early teens, I still sought my mother's approval. One day when I asked her if she would be proud of me if I became a performer, she asked, "Shelley, do you really want to know what would make me proud of you?"

"Yes, I do," I said.

She looked into my eyes and in a most loving way said, "If you become a responsible and caring adult who contributes to rather than takes from the world, I will be very proud of you no matter what you choose to do, and I will know that I have done well as your mother."

Some years later, my mother made a sampler that she framed and displayed in our home. After she died of cancer in 1982, I inherited her wonderfully creative piece with its life-changing message:

What we are is
God's gift to us.
What we become is
our gift to God.

The sampler now hangs in my office as a reminder of how I learned who I really am and how I wish to live in light of that knowledge. It reminds me of God's gift to me and of the gift I want to return to Him. It is the inspiration for this book.

For some years, clients and friends had been encouraging me to write about the experiences that inspired my faith and shaped my therapeutic principles. For most of my adult life, however, I had imposed a paralyzing nemesis upon myself regarding my writing abilities. In fact, I developed performance skills for speaking engagements so I could run from writing. I thought that writing down my thoughts would reveal my "stupidity" to others.

How was it possible to have such inaccurate, self-defeating thoughts? I had been a professional actor and singer in the United States and abroad. I had worked as a public safety officer, a certified firefighter, an emergency technician II, and a commercial fisherwoman. I had earned a physician's assistant degree in family medicine and taught basic medicine to rural indigenous Alaskans.

Yet my life experiences also included childhood sexual molestation, psychological abuse, debilitating allergies, and autoimmune illness. My self-perception grew from those experiences, not from my accomplishments, and for years I thought of myself as inferior—helpless, unintelligent, and ugly. These negative thoughts resulted in chronic illness, seven major surgeries, divorce, and an irreversible decision not to have children.

> *No one can make you feel inferior without your consent.*
>
> —ELEANOR ROOSEVELT

I had to learn that "what we become" is the result of our thoughts, words, and actions, as well as our willingness to strive toward excellence regardless of the discouragement we encounter on life's journey or the transgressions we commit along the way. When I learned that, I was finally ready to break through my self-imposed writing block and begin to share the experiences that have provided me with opportunities to learn how the mind, faith, and prayer can promote optimum healing, love, and life.

Through God's grace and forgiveness, I now write to you as a victor, not a victim. With gratitude and humility, I share my healing triumph. I pray that *The Sampler* will support the healing of your mind, body, and spirit so that *you too* may live a victor's life.

Part One

Choosing Life

Chapter One

A Matter of Life and Death

*"God so loved the world that he gave
his one and only Son,
that whoever believes in him shall not
perish but have eternal life."*

John 3:16

On the day we are born, our bodies begin to move toward death. Unless we deliberately choose life, our spirits will do the same. When God sent His Son to die in our place, He provided us with a way to choose living over dying. Yet even when we have chosen Christ, and even though we know we will live forever with Him, many of us think in ways that reflect a dying spirit, one that keeps us from enjoying the fullness of life Christ has promised us.

That was once true for me. For many years, my negative, fearful thinking created "death to my spirit." It took a near-death experience and the subsequent challenges of neck surgery and cancer for me to realize that I was focused on dying instead of on living.

> *He not busy being born is busy dying.*
>
> — BOB DYLAN

DYING WHILE LIVING

On April 3, 1998, my colon ruptured. The contents of my intestines spilled into my abdominal cavity, and I bled internally for over four hours before I arrived at the emergency room of Cottage Grove Hospital. By then, my veins had collapsed. I had no measurable blood pressure.

I was dying.

No more pain. At last, no more pain. The movements of those around me slowed and became meaningless. Their loud, frantic voices faded away to unintelligible murmurs. My body seemed to float upward, and an indescribable sense of peace filled my entire being.

"It's okay. All is right," I said, though my lips did not move and no one could hear me. Unafraid, I let go. *Beautiful.*

Suddenly I was startled by a mild shock, followed by a soft, warm pressure in the palm of my left hand, the only place I felt any sensation. I squeezed lightly.

What is this?

I realized that I was gripping the index and middle fingers of my husband's right hand. I felt his palm and thumb curl around my hand and hold it tightly. I didn't want to leave that serene place, but Ken's loving touch was pulling me back. My body became heavier.

Without my willing them to, my eyes opened, and I caught Ken's penetrating glance across my body at Terry Kendrick, the ER physician. Terry's hands trembled as he tried to insert an IV into the vein just below my collarbone, dangerously close to my lung.

All of a sudden, I desperately wanted to keep living. I wanted to continue sharing life with the man whose life force was beckoning me to stay. Ken's abiding faith and love had already helped me heal from earlier health challenges, and we shared a powerful and mutual willingness to grow in our relationship.

God, this can't be the end yet. Please, I want to stay. Ken, can you hear me? Keep holding on to me. I want to stay here with you.

I wanted to encourage and calm Terry, but again my lips would not move. Ken is a doctor and had often worked in this ER. On some level, I knew that now all he could do was pray that Terry would succeed in pulling me back.

Suddenly, energy filled my lungs, allowing me to

whisper, "It's okay, everyone. We can all relax now. Everything will be all right. We remember everything we learned in our medical training. We can do this. Trust in God."

Terry's hands steadied, and moments later a searing pain ripped through my insides, sucking words and breath out of my mouth. The central line was in, and my body was responding to the lifesaving fluids. The indescribable, overwhelming pain returned. I was definitely back.

I began to writhe and moan, "Oh, dear God, the pain. Will someone please give me something for the pain? Dear heavenly Father, help me through this! Ken?"

An ambulance rushed me the twenty-five miles to Sacred Heart Medical Center in Eugene. After six hours of surgery, as I awakened from the general anesthetic, the surgeon leaned down and whispered in my ear, "You now have a colostomy, Shelley. We've removed a portion of your lower colon. The surgery went well. If we can control this infection, you'll be out of the hospital in about ten days. Six weeks from now I'll reverse the procedure and reconnect your colon."

Through the grace of God, the prayers of family and friends, and a vigorous rehabilitation program, I rapidly recovered. Four weeks after my colon ruptured, I comfortably stood upright on stage and sang a solo with my beloved singing group of eleven years, the Eugene Vocal Arts Ensemble. Of all the wonderful and loving comments the members of this talented group made to me, my favorite remains, "Shelley is back—as a semi-colon!"

Two years later, I had surgery to fuse three vertebrae in my neck. During that procedure, the surgeons discovered metastatic thyroid cancer. Six weeks later, they removed my thyroid and the lymph glands in my neck. After surgery I had radioactive isotope treatments and took large amounts of thyroid hormone to suppress the growth of the remaining seven tumors.

My near-death experience, neck surgery, and treatment for cancer brought me to a turning point in my life. For too long I had focused on dying while living. Now I would focus on living while dying.

> *The phrase "being born" is used for beginning to be something different from what one was before, while "dying" means ceasing to be the same.*
>
> —OVID

LIVING WHILE DYING

In my journey toward healing, as a maturing Christian I found solace in entering into a new covenant with God— one that promises His grace and forgiveness. It took me many years to understand and accept these notions. *Could years of being harmed and harming others really be undone by a simple act of faith?*

The answer is not that the harm can be undone, but that harm can be both redeemed and redeeming. Forgiving and being forgiven have been essential parts of my journey to healing.

Do I have regrets? Yes, some. I still regret that some of my poor choices harmed others. I have made amends with those willing to receive apologies. Most have forgiven me, though not all. However, I no longer have any regrets about the harm done to me. With time, I came to understand that my experiences were not punishments, but challenging parts of God's personal training program for me. Just as a runner must clear the hurdles to win a race, I had to meet those challenges to be able to write to you as a victor, not as a victim.

The healing process, which meant substantially less time with clients, was a wonderful blessing, for it gave me the time I needed to finish this book. Meanwhile, I have enjoyed the most healthful and energetic time in my life. When I started writing, I still had seven cancerous tumors. Eighteen months later, a full-body radioisotope scan revealed that all signs of them had disappeared. And, although there are other aspects of my health that may lead some to say I am not *cured,* the fact that I feel and look so well convinces me that, regardless of my physical state, I am *healed.*

Since you are reading this book, I expect that you also have a desire to live while you're dying—to discover your God-given gifts and become a gift worthy of returning to Him. Right now the fulfillment of these aspirations may feel far away, just as the finish line must seem to a runner at the starting block. No matter. Every journey has a beginning, and we reach the end by taking the first step and then continuing to move in the right direction. As we begin the therapeutic journey to healing, I ask you take the first step—I ask you to make a commitment to change.

> *The journey of a thousand miles*
> *must begin with a single step.*
>
> —LAO-TZU

Chapter Two

Commitment to Change through Therapy

*"I tell you the truth, unless you change
and become like little children,
you will never enter the kingdom of heaven."*

MATTHEW 18:3

The purpose of therapy is not to rid us of our emotions. It is to help us understand and accept them so they enhance rather than diminish our lives. Therapy helps us to grow up and become mature, loving adults.

Feelings rule an immature person. Childish people act impulsively, without considering the impact their actions will have on the moment or on the future. Such behavior can devastate us and destroy our relationships. Mature people, on the other hand, take responsibility for their behavior regardless of their emotional state.

Being childlike is not the same as being childish. We want to become mature without losing our childlikeness, for that is what keeps us in awe of such wonders as a beautifully written book, a gorgeous sunset, or a stunning musical performance. It is what ushers us into the presence of God and allows Him to begin to grow us up by conforming us to the image of His Son. How can therapy help us grow into a childlike maturity?

> *When I grow up, I want to be a little boy.*
>
> — WILL FOLEY

INNER WISDOM

When I ask clients what they expect from therapy, some say something like "I'm not going to let him or her do that to me any longer." It is misguided to think that we can control life or the people in it. The only thing we can control is how we perceive and respond to our life experiences. What we can do is to make a commitment to change. But in order to change, we have to identify our needs and the steps we must take to reach them. Often people have trouble doing that.

Some clients say things like "I don't like this about myself" or "I don't want to do that anymore." These responses underscore a sincere motivation to become healthier by changing. However, if you focus only on what you don't want, you are unlikely to get what you do want.

Other clients state their expectations positively. They say they "want to be happy," "wish to feel more confident," or "would like to get rid of pain." Yet when I ask what causes their unhappiness, lack of confidence, or pain and what steps they feel they must take to change their situations, many answer, "I don't know."

Through the years, I have found that most people do know what they want. What they really hope to do is to strengthen their self-love and become more loving toward others. They seek therapy because they feel incapable of giving or receiving love. This need is often difficult for people to express because loving oneself first is often equated with self-centeredness. But that is not so. We all want to love and be loved, and self-love allows us to love others and others to love us.

My clients have also taught me that they know what they need to do to become more loving. Either they have come to believe they don't know, or they do not want to know—but they do know. Therapy can help us tap in to our inner wisdom.

BAD HABITS

Therapy can also reveal the habits that prevent us from taking the steps we need to take to change. Most of the time people come to therapy because they don't like how they feel. Clients often tell me, "You know, if I just felt better and had more confidence, maybe I would have the courage to do things differently." Yet love and all other feelings are secondary to how we behave, not the other way around. How we feel is the result of how we behave. We begin to feel better only when we begin to do things differently.

Sometimes it takes my clients a moment to grasp this concept. With their permission, I ask them to close their eyes and take a few deep breaths to induce a state of relaxation. Next I ask them to imagine a place where they experience happiness or safety. I ask them for a signal, such as a raised hand or a nod, when they find such a place. Then I ask if they are willing to imagine a scene where they experience something that causes sadness or anxiety. Again I wait for a signal. Finally, I ask them to return to the first place.

Three observations can be made about this exercise. First, most clients successfully complete it. Second, they recognize that there is a significant relationship between what they think and how they feel. Third, many find it very difficult to leave the place that makes them feel unhappy and return to the one that makes them feel content. Remaining in negative thoughts is easier because it has become a habit. With motivation and vigilance, a commitment to change through therapy can reverse that habit.

Replacing old behaviors with new behaviors is no easy task. Here is a statement I share with clients to help them focus on their goals: "I am not doing this to make my life easier, but to make my life better." Fortunately, when we make our lives better, we often make them easier as well.

When making a commitment to change, there is a caution. We want to strive for excellence, not perfection. During challenging times, striving for excellence may mean simply making the effort to get out of bed and greet the day. When we strive for excellence, we set goals that are high, but also attainable. When we make mistakes, we correct and learn from them, and we are happy knowing we did our best. When we strive for perfection, on the other hand, we think we can be happy only if we are the best, so we set unrealistic goals and dwell on our mistakes. The only way we are to strive to be "perfect" is in the sense of "mature"—and striving for that kind of perfection almost always involves pain and suffering.

> *Pain is the breaking of the shell that*
> *encloses our understanding.*
>
> —KAHLIL GIBRAN

PAIN AND SUFFERING

The first of the Buddha's four "noble truths" is "There is suffering." As human beings, we cannot avoid it. If we engage in life, we will suffer. Suffering is not a sign that God has singled us out for punishment. And while it is not personal, the way we handle it is. Therapy can help us learn to avoid self-inflicted suffering caused by ignorance, fear, selfishness, or lack of faith. In this, God is our personal resource for wisdom and strength. When we choose to make a commitment to change and become willing to learn from our suffering, we set ourselves on a journey that ends when we present Him with the gift of our mature, childlike self.

When we accept suffering as a necessary part of growth, our pain diminishes, and our willingness to continue our inner journey increases. When suffering drives us toward actualizing our potential as human beings, we learn to celebrate the crisis of change as an opportunity to change.

Once clients begin to experience positive results through therapy, I share this paradox with them: "The good news about therapy is that once you have grown up and out of the old self, you can never comfortably fit back into your old self again. The bad news about therapy is that once you have grown up and out of the old self, you can never comfortably fit back into your old self again."

It's rather like hermit crabs when the time comes for them to grow. They have to leave their old shells and scurry about totally naked until they find larger ones. Over time, they become quite adept at taking this risk. It takes little imagination to picture their plight if they were to remain in their old shells!

Once you've set out on the road to healing, there should be no turning back. Whether we accept it or not, change is a constant throughout life. All of us who want to make our lives better recognize on some level that to be fully alive and well, we must change. Yet it is often the case that we become motivated to act only when our suffering becomes greater than our fear of changing.

The emotion of suffering ceases to be suffering as soon as we form a clear and precise picture of it.

— SPINOZA

Chapter Three

Overcoming Fear

"Fear not, for I have redeemed you;
I have called you by your name; You are Mine.
When you pass through the waters, I will be with you;
And through the rivers, they shall not overflow you."

Isaiah 43:1–2, NKJV

The fear of the unknown can often be stronger than the desire to escape a difficult situation. For those unfamiliar with the benefits of therapy, the prospect of exploring their inner world may be threatening. They may fear they will lose control if they admit they need help, or they may fear exposing the "shame" of their past.

Clients often have deep-seated fears they aren't even aware of. That is true for all of us. When we become aware of them—often through an act of courage in the face of fear—we see how little there really is to be afraid of. I learned that late one stormy afternoon in October of 1996.

> *Fear is a question: What are you afraid of, and why?*
> *Just as the seed of health is in illness, because illness*
> *contains information, your fears are a treasure house*
> *of self-knowledge if you explore them.*
>
> — MARILYN FERGUSON

THE CROSSING

The Willamette River had overflowed its banks, and I received an alarming phone call from the owners of the stable where we boarded my little Arab gelding, Foxfire. The stable and the road to the barn were flooded. Ken and I threw on our rain gear, jumped in our Explorer, and raced to the scene. To get to the barn we had to cross a cornfield, but by now it was a hundred-foot-wide expanse of rushing water filled with debris. The road across the field dipped five feet in the middle, creating a whirlpool that made it too dangerous to try to cross by truck.

Attempts to rescue the thirty-five horses remaining in the barn had been called off two hours earlier. Now the search and rescue team told us that the floodgates upriver would soon be opened. Even more water would be coming our way.

My heart was racing. I couldn't stand the thought of

what would happen to Foxfire. Out of Ken's earshot I convinced a member of the rescue crew to take me across by boat. He handed me a life vest and ten minutes later dropped me off in calmer water on the other side of the river. For forty-five minutes I sloshed the remaining one-quarter mile to the stable in water up to my thighs. By the time I arrived it was totally dark.

The inside arena and stalls were flooded. I called for Foxy. He saw me and whinnied. "Good boy," I said. "Easy, Foxy." He stood perfectly still, though the water was rushing above his knees. I fought back tears and the sickening feeling churning in my stomach.

Keep calm, Shelley. You must keep calm.

I made my way through the pitch black to the tack room. My compulsion to keep things organized and always in the same place now paid off. I immediately located his tack, grabbed it, and made my way back to his stall. By the time I reached him, I was too cold and exhausted to get up on his back. My toes and fingers were numb, and asthma was making every breath a challenge.

What am I going to do now? How much time do I have left before they open the floodgates? Will the water sweep us away? I should have told Ken what I was planning to do.

Shut up, Shelley! Think. Pray.

To my amazement and relief, I now saw that four volunteers had waded into the barn shortly after I did. They yelled through the darkness and pouring rain for Foxy and me to wait while they caught some horses. When they returned, one of them gave me a leg up onto Foxfire. Like me, Foxy was shaking from the wet and cold. Once mounted, we formed a caravan.

Before we left the barn, I told the volunteers about the hazardous deep section of the crossing. We would need to stay upstream from the telephone poles lining the road, for running alongside the road on the downstream side of the poles was a long, deep ditched filled with thick blackberry bushes.

Silhouetted by blazing headlights on the opposite bank, the five of us worked our way to the end of the gravel lane and prepared to make the crossing. I looked over at the lights, searching for Ken, but I couldn't make out anything in the glare. The first two riders started across, their horses swimming. They were moving forward but also slightly downstream.

I don't know how I could have had any adrenaline left, but more kicked in as I urged Foxfire forward. Soon his legs were swept out from under him. The current was pushing us closer and closer to the telephone poles. I leaned forward, hugged his neck, squeezed my legs, and shouted, "Come on Foxfire. Come on boy…. Go, Foxy…. Go, boy! You can do it…. Go, boy, go!"

On we went until we passed the two larger and

stronger horses in front of us. We pulled out of the water on the other side and stood in the mud, exhausted but jubilant. Ken took the reins and helped me off Foxfire. Everyone else was looking at the last two horse and riders, who had been swept away behind us. The rescuers grabbed the riders, but the two pregnant mares were caught in the raging current and swiftly taken downstream.

There is a happy ending. The floodgates upriver were never opened, and the thirty horses still in the barn were saved. The two mares returned to the barn four days later and eventually delivered healthy, full-term foals.

This experience taught me something important about myself. As I was shouting at Foxfire to keep going, I had looked up and seen the people on shore watching us. *Oh my God,* I thought, *they must think I'm a total idiot for risking my life for a horse!* During the entire adventure, I don't remember having any fear of dying. I just remember having an uncontrollable desire to save my horse. It was only later that I felt afraid—afraid of ridicule and rejection—although there was no evidence at all, then or later, to indicate what the onlookers were really thinking.

FEAR
False Evidence Appearing Real

This story emphasizes a deep-seated fear many of us have—the fear that others may perceive us in a negative light and reject us. That fear is very real to many clients at the start of therapy. In helping them get beyond the roadblock of fear, I review with them that feelings are secondary to behaviors. Then I share two metaphors to help them feel safer during the journey.

YOU ARE THE DRIVER

The first metaphor I use involves a car and driver. I tell my clients they are about to travel into unfamiliar territory and ask them to think about planning a safe journey. Making the travel plan begins with selecting a car with a good engine, responsive steering, and reliable brakes. They may want to test drive a few cars before making their selection. Once they find a suitable car and map out their route, they can begin the journey.

In a safe therapeutic journey, therapy is the car and the client is the driver. With both therapist and client observing appropriate boundaries and the rules of the road, the driver determines the speed of therapy, whether to drive on a rugged side road or a smooth freeway, when to turn or stop, and whether to continue the journey. When clients discover their excellent driving skills, they feel encouraged and safe.

I AM THE MIRROR

I use another therapeutic metaphor to help clients understand the important benefits of communicating openly and honestly. As a caring therapist, my responsibility is to hold up a mirror that reflects how clients see themselves, based on their experiences—real or imagined, intentional or unintentional. I reflect to them what they tell me they see. When I do, clients frequently see a film of negative thoughts clouding their mirror. In successful therapy, they learn to wipe away the film so they can see how truly wonderful they are. This enables them to see their past experiences as *building* blocks, not *stumbling* blocks.

Feeling confident is not a prerequisite for change. We promote confident feelings through courageous actions. When we act to overcome our fears, our confidence grows. It is an act of courage, in spite of fear, that wins the day. *How we feel is the result of how we behave.*

Many of our fears are tissue-paper thin, and a single courageous step would carry us clear through them.

—BRENDAN FRASER

LIFE-ENHANCING CONCEPTS RIGHT AT YOUR FINGERTIPS

In the rest of *The Sampler,* I discuss concepts that can help change behaviors and the feelings they invoke. I have developed two acronyms to facilitate remembering these concepts—HIRTL and TRACK. Many of my clients have found them useful and have urged me to write them down.

HIRTL stands for the hurdles we must clear on the journey to healing. It can be shown graphically as your *left* hand with its palm facing *away from* your body. Starting with the little finger, we strive for **h**onesty, **i**ntegrity, and **r**espect, which are increasingly higher hurdles. Once we clear them and learn to **t**rust, we slide into the cradle of **l**ove. TRACK is represented as the fingers of your *right* hand facing *toward* your body. Starting again with the little finger, we strive for **t**ruth, **r**esponsibility, **a**ttitude, **c**haracter, and **k**nowledge—the *right* things we need to stay on track on our journey. Here are ten life-enhancing concepts—right at your fingertips!

Part Two

Clearing
the Hurdles

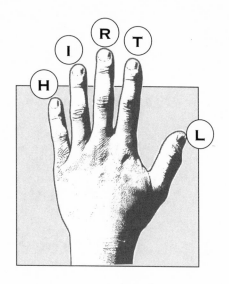

———— ⟨✺⟩ ————

Chapter Four

Honesty

Speaking the truth in love,
we will in all things grow up
into him who is the Head,
that is, Christ.

EPHESIANS 4:15

The **h** in HIRTL refers to honesty. We begin the healing journey by learning to honestly examine our reasons for doing what we do. The purpose of this self-examination is to discern and understand our motives, not judge them. As we better understand what motivates our words and actions, we can begin to comprehend the motivations of others and thus prevent needless misunderstandings. The first time I really understood this was when I realized that my mother was dying.

> *This above all: to thine own self be true.*
> *And it must follow as the night the day:*
> *Thou canst not then be false to any man.*
>
> —WILLIAM SHAKESPEARE

DECEPTIVE SELF-TALK

The summer before I was to leave for medical training, my mother was diagnosed with a highly aggressive form of cancer. When it came time to leave for school, I didn't want to go. She was awaiting multiple surgeries and radiation therapy, and I wanted to be with her. But she was adamant that I not lose the opportunity for this education and made me promise to go. I promised, but I was prepared to leave at a moment's notice if she didn't improve or if she needed me in any way.

At first, it appeared she was winning her bout with cancer. During our frequent talks on the phone, she sounded just like the person I had always known. Her sense of humor remained strong, she had a positive outlook, and she radiated love for everyone around her. Some months into the treatments, however, her doctor called to tell me that she was failing to respond to treatment. He thought she wouldn't live much longer than six more months.

I rushed home. When I walked into her bedroom, my heart sank. I ached and my throat constricted as I put my arms around her frail, shrinking body. She greeted me cheerfully and then chastised me for leaving school.

What I cared about most at this point was being with her and talking candidly with her about her feelings about dying. I felt we *had* to have this discussion. Although I felt ill prepared, a few days later I found the courage to broach the subject. My mother was deeply agitated and said that she did not want to talk about it. I didn't know what to say or do. I had wanted to help and comfort her, and I had failed miserably. I was devastated.

A friend gave me the name of a grief counselor, and I made an appointment. The first thing the counselor asked me was why I had come to therapy. I told her that I needed to find an effective way to talk to my mother about death and dying. She then asked me what my motive was for wanting to do this. I told her that I wanted to comfort my mother and help allay her fears about death. I began to cry.

"Are you sure that is the real reason you came to see me?" the therapist asked kindly.

"Well certainly," I said, still in tears. "I love my mother. She is suffering, and she is angry. If she could only talk about it, she would feel much better. But she won't talk about her cancer. She needs to do this, but I can't help her. I feel so helpless and worthless."

The therapist very gently said, "Shelley, can you understand that the true motivation for your visit comes from *your* need to be comforted and *your* need to allay your own fears about death and dying? It is important that you understand your real motivation here. If it is truly your intention to help and comfort your mother, may I suggest that you allow her to lead the way? This is her time. She will need you to accept whatever way she chooses to handle this. Be a good listener. Allow *her* to initiate the conversations."

I realized that the therapist was right. What I was really saying was, "If she could only talk about it, *I* would feel much better." What were my own feelings? I didn't even know. I had yet to develop a deep, Christian perspective on death and dying. My description of my motives was deceptive self-talk. And it had the exact opposite effect of what I had wanted. Instead of bringing me closer to my dying mother, it had shut me off from her.

Our lives improve only when we take chances— and the first and most difficult risk we can take is to be honest with ourselves.

—WALTER ANDERSON

HONEST SELF-TALK

Honesty requires us to stop and pay attention to our thoughts and actions. Once we honestly look at our motives, we can decide on a course of action based on honest self-talk—a course that will help us build successful, transparent relationships.

I once had a client who had experienced a difficult, painful divorce. She began dating a man and, after getting to know him, expressed an interest in pursuing an exclusive relationship with him. When the man didn't respond as she expected, she felt rejected and unlovable. However, with honest self-examination during therapy, she acknowledged that her motives had been rooted in soothing her loneliness and pain, not in building a loving and lasting relationship.

How can we know when we are not being honest with ourselves? There are two red flags that commonly signal a need for self-examination.

RED FLAGS

The first red flag is anger. Because anger is often considered inappropriate, we sometimes feel ashamed when we become angry. Yet in itself anger is a legitimate emotion, one that prepares us to protect ourselves in the face of fear, pain, or frustration. Asking ourselves what frightens, hurts, or frustrates us is the key to discovering what is fueling our anger.

Honestly admitting the underlying cause of our anger enables us to channel it appropriately, as Marianne learned during her sixth session in therapy. That day, she walked into my office, plopped down on the couch, and began to cry.

"I am so angry right now," she said. "On my way here, I got a call from my husband. He said he didn't think I handled myself well when we were talking to the doctor about our ADHD child. I was so angry I hung up on him. Now I bet he's *really* angry with me. I don't want to go home. And I'm *not* going home—at least for several hours. That will teach him."

I asked Marianne if she remembered the three emotions that usually trigger feelings of anger and if any of them had preceded hers. She realized she had at first felt hurt because her husband criticized her, and then afraid because she had hung up on him. After therapy she went directly home to have an honest talk with him about the episode.

Anger is a signal, and one worth listening to.

—HARRIET LERNER

We are not bad if we feel angry. However, if we don't recognize the source of our anger, we can sometimes behave in ways that hurt the people we care for. Learning to consciously choose healthy behavior even when we feel angry can help us avoid hurting others and ourselves.

The second behavior that signals our need for self-examination is manipulation. Marianne's threat to not return home is a classic example of the kind of manipulation that destroys relationships. Until she got to the root of her anger, she mistakenly believed that punishing her offending husband would make her feel less vulnerable.

Acting out in anger is not the only behavior that can be designed to "get something" from someone else. Kind behavior can be manipulative as well. When we try to fulfill our desires or make ourselves feel better through insincere charm or false generosity, we are walking on dangerous ground. Even when we get what it is we think we want, we lose respect for those we manipulate. More importantly, we lose respect for ourselves.

When we can honestly evaluate the motives for what we think, say, and do, and then act on that knowledge, we have cleared the first hurdle. Honesty enhances our authenticity and prepares us for the next hurdle—integrity.

Chapter Five

Integrity

I know, my God,
that you test the heart
and are pleased with integrity.

1 CHRONICLES 29:17

We often use the word *integrity* as if it meant the same
thing as *honesty*, but there is much more to it. The word
has the same root as the words *integer* and *entire*, both of
which convey the idea of something that is whole, complete, and undivided. We cannot be mature without
integrity, and to have it, all of us at some point have to
choose how we are going perceive the events of our lives.
Are we going to look at them in a way that makes us *bit-
ter*—or in a way that makes us *better*?

BITTER...OR BETTER?

One morning about six months after Ken and I were married, I found him sitting on the stairs, bent over and holding his head in his hands. Alarmed at his unusual behavior, I sat down beside him and asked what was troubling him. At first he said nothing, but after a few minutes he admitted that he was concerned about our relationship. He wanted to know if I loved him.

I was stunned. How could he doubt my love for him?

Ken told me that if he touched me while I was sleeping, I would move to the edge of our bed and hang my arm, leg, and head over the side. Afraid that I would fall out of bed and hurt myself, he had stopped reaching for me.

"I think something inside of you is telling you to run from me," he said.

I had never told Ken that my father had molested me when I was a child. Now, with some trepidation, I did. He had to know that I wasn't running from *him*. He had to know how much I loved him and how desirable he was to me in every way.

I told Ken that I was willing to take whatever steps were necessary to overcome my flashbacks and anxiety. I put my desire for a healthy marriage ahead of my fear and shame, and with the help of therapy and prayer, I learned to remove unhealthy images from my mind and replace them with healthy ones.

During therapy I came to understand that my father had not intended to harm me. Abused as a child himself, he felt inadequate as an adult and so tried to satisfy his sexual desires with a child. Alcohol also played a role. My parents began drinking every night before dinner and continued until bedtime. It was only during these extended cocktail hours, when alcohol lowered his inhibitions, that my father molested me. I believed I had genuinely forgiven him, yet the ghosts of the past still haunted me, and periodically I became angry.

"What he did to me was *bad*," I would say to my therapist, "and it has affected my entire life. I chose not to have children because of it. Why bring children into this world? So they can feel as awful inside as I have?"

My therapist knew that we had to find a way for me to accept my past, so she asked if I could identify any of my father's behaviors that were positive and loving. Both of us were surprised at how many I came up with.

"But," I said, "that still doesn't undo what he did to me."

Then she asked me if, when those thoughts surfaced and I couldn't calm my angry feelings, I would be willing to think the following:

The positive things he did do not change those that were wrong and hurtful. The wrong and hurtful things he did do not change those that were positive and loving. Is my glass half-full or half-empty? The glass is both. My perspective determines how I feel. I can choose to feel empty for the rest of my life, or I can choose to feel full.

Choosing to see the glass as half-empty brings death to our spirit; choosing to see it as half-full brings life. Choosing to focus on where we are today and where we are headed instead of dwelling on the past keeps us from being double-minded and gets us over the hurdle of integrity.

How do we know when we have cleared the hurdle? What behaviors demonstrate that we are no longer divided against ourselves, but that we are becoming whole, mature people? We can tell we have taken this giant step toward maturity when, first, we no longer blame others or complain about where we find ourselves in life and when, second, we keep our word.

Our life is what our thoughts make it.

— MARCUS AURELIUS

NOT BLAMING OR COMPLAINING

Many of us keep our thoughts and feelings well hidden—at times even from ourselves—so we may not consider ourselves blamers. We also often fail to recognize that complaining is a form of blaming. An honest self-examination will reveal if you need work in this area. Get in touch with your feelings. Do you feel jealous, sorry for yourself, put upon? Listen to yourself. Do you hear yourself saying things like "It's not fair," "It's your fault," "If only he hadn't done that"? This kind of self-talk is a sign that you are blaming others for what's going on in your life.

In whatever form it takes, blaming destroys love by blocking forgiveness. A fresh look at our beliefs can help us break the habit of blaming. For example, when clients struggle to get past issues stemming from relationships with their parents, I ask them, "Do you really believe that your parents sat down before your birth and made a detailed list of all the things they could do to make your life miserable?" This comment usually elicits an understanding smile—and the process of forgiving their parents begins.

When we stop blaming and complaining, we stop making our situation worse and start making it better. And how invigorating to discover that when we quit blaming, we feel better!

KEEPING OUR WORD

Keeping our word simply means doing what we say we're going to do. When you give someone your word, do you keep it?

All of us can remember times when we have promised someone something and then failed to keep the promise because circumstances just didn't allow us to follow through. At such times, we usually feel bad about having let someone down. However, we don't need to feel guilty. We all know that "life happens." But if we habitually don't make good on our promises, we suffer a loss of integrity—and that can have devastating consequences for any relationship.

> *Write injuries in dust, benefits in marble.*
>
> —BENJAMIN FRANKLIN

For some months, I worked with a married couple in their midthirties who didn't keep their word. Habitually breaking the promises they made to each other eventually caused a complete breakdown in communication. Neither wanted to hear the other's point of view. This marriage was in the emergency room on external life support—and fading fast. As a last resort, they came to therapy.

In seeking professional help, they were in essence promising each other that they would identify and change the behaviors that were destroying their relationship. During the first sessions, however, they displayed little respect for each other. One partner consistently arrived late, and then refused to participate. Once the unpunctual partner *did* agree to take part, the other one constantly interrupted. From the start, they were breaking the implicit promise to do what was necessary to save their marriage. Without realizing it, they were perpetuating the pattern of failing to keep their word to each other.

To break the impasse, we arranged a block of therapy sessions in which they promised to show up on time and do exercises designed to enhance their listening skills. Rather than verbally striking out when their emotions were volatile, they practiced writing down their feelings and sharing them when they were calm. They also listed each other's positive aspects and the reasons they wanted to stay in the marriage, as opposed to why they wanted to leave. Gradually, they began to see the glass as half-full instead of half-empty.

As a result of keeping their word to show up on time and do the exercises, this couple discovered the importance of following through with the behaviors that would help them build a relationship based on integrity. They saved their relationship and now continue to mature together.

The key to integrity is choosing to take responsibility for *our* thoughts, *our* words, and *our* actions, regardless of what others do to us or how we feel about it. We can get to that point by being honest with ourselves and becoming willing to identify what lies behind our failure to keep our promises or our propensity to blame. Learning to report our challenging or disturbing discoveries instead of complaining about them enables us to engage in positive behaviors despite our feelings. That makes us people of integrity and positions us to clear the hurdle of respect.

Integrity is the recognition of the fact that you cannot fake your consciousness, just as honesty is the recognition of the fact that you cannot fake existence.

—AYN RAND

Chapter Six

Respect

Whatever is true, whatever is noble, whatever is right,
whatever is pure, whatever is lovely, whatever is admirable—
if anything is excellent or praiseworthy—
think about such things.

PHILIPPIANS 4:8

Remember the left hand graphic? By the time we come to the third finger, we have reached the highest hurdle—respect. It's the highest because acting respectfully requires us to control what we think and what we say—and that requires a lot of self-discipline.

Sooner or later, the thoughts we allow to occupy our mind will determine our actions. That, in turn, will determine how we feel. (Remember: Our feelings are the result of our actions.) Thoughts drive behavior, and behavior drives feelings. If we think negative thoughts, we act in negative ways, and as a result, we feel bad. Standing between our thoughts and our behavior are our words. Words have the power to help us choose healthy thoughts over unhealthy ones. The healthier our words, the more respect we show for our body, mind, and spirit, and the better we feel.

Wonderful is the healthiest, most loving, and most respectful word in my vocabulary. I can use it regardless of how I feel, and so can you. If you use it, I promise you will feel...*wonder full!*

> *The mind grows by what it feeds on.*
>
> —JOSIAH GILBERT HOLLAND

FULL OF WONDER

I was practicing family medicine in Junction City, Oregon, while hobbling around on crutches as I recovered from a fracture to my right leg. Toward the end of one day, I was experiencing considerable discomfort. Steve, a fellow practitioner new to the clinic, kindly asked, "Shelley, how are you doing? In some pain?"

"A bit challenged," I replied, "but I am actually wonderful. Thank you for asking."

"Come on, Shelley," Steve said. "Get real. *Wonderful*

doesn't sound like an honest reply. You look like you're in pain."

I smiled. "What does *wonderful* mean to you?" I asked.

"It means everything is fantastic," he said. " No problems and life is great."

"I like your definition," I said, "but mine is a little different. To me, the word *wonderful* means full of wonder— wonder full. As we speak, I am full of wonder that my leg bone is busy healing itself. I feel better when I think of it in that way."

The way we speak can earn us respect or disrespect, from ourselves as well as others. We learn an important skill when we talk in a life-enhancing manner. Changing the way we use words can create imagery capable of increasing or diminishing our joy or our pain. Some words enhance our energy; others drain us of it.

FOUR-LETTER WORDS

I refrain from using the word *pain* because of its power, and I suggest to my clients that they use the word *discomfort* instead. Until the change becomes habit, I suggest they say, "I have a pain," rather than "I am in pain." Saying that we are *in pain* creates the same kind of mind picture as saying that we are *in God*. Whatever we are *in* is clearly bigger and more powerful than we are. Being in God is a good thing; being in pain is not. If we see pain as larger than we are, we can easily conclude that we are powerless to change our state without medication. If we say that we *have pain,* however, we create the image that we are larger than it and therefore can control it.

> *Say not God is in my heart,*
> *but rather I am in the heart of God.*
>
> —KAHLIL GIBRAN

Some years ago, while practicing family medicine, I sought a technique that would quickly and accurately evaluate patients who urgently needed care. When we undergo serious injury or illness, we exist in highly suggestive states. Quickly decreasing feelings of pain and fear can help stabilize patients, so I brought into the clinical setting the skills I had learned and practiced on myself.

After an evaluation and reassurance, I focus my patients' attention. Next I ask, "On a scale from one to ten, with one being the most comfortable and ten the least comfortable, which number best describes the way you feel?" The scale helps validate their perception of pain while sending a message to their brain to evaluate their body's level of *comfort* instead of its level of *pain.*

Using the number patients choose, I ask them to imagine holding a control knob numbered one to ten over the area of discomfort. When they have done that, I ask if they are willing to turn the dial to a slightly higher number, even though doing so may mean greater discomfort. When patients agree and succeed in raising the number, they realize they can also use their mind to lower the number to a more comfortable level. Once they have successfully completed this exercise, they are aware of the tremendous power their thoughts can have on their bodies. This in turn prepares them to tap into one of God's grand gifts—prayer, a natural way to relieve the challenges of discomfort.

Pain is only one of the words we should avoid when we are striving for respect. *Can't* is another. Using it suggests that something beyond our control is preventing us from accomplishing a particular task and makes us sound like victims. Admittedly, all of us find that there are some things we literally are unable to do. A newborn can't walk; a man can't bear a child; a blind person can't see. Normally, however, we can do just about anything we choose to do. If you make comments like "I just can't cut down on my workload to rest and heal," you're not being honest. The point is: Yes, you can.

We always have options. What keeps us from choosing to exercise one is our fear that there will be an undesirable consequence if we do. It's more honest to say, "I *won't* cut down on my workload to rest and heal because we won't have enough money." Stating it this way can also lead you to take greater responsibility for the outcome because it begs the question, "Is 'enough' money really more important than my health?"

Hate is a lethal four-letter word. Anytime we use or hear the word *hate* to describe our feelings about anyone or anything, we not only create negative energy that can hinder our immune system, but we also show a lack of respect for ourselves and others.

Other examples of deadly expressions include: "You're killing me," "I'm dying to know," "You make me sick," and "You're a pain in the neck." In addition to avoiding such "four-letter" phrases, you can substitute active, positive words for passive, negative ones.

> *Where we do not respect, we cease to love.*
>
> —BENJAMIN DISRAELI

WONDERFUL WORDS OF LIFE

Here are some ways to exchange debilitating phrases for life-giving language that gains respect for ourselves and others.

Instead of "I am *worried* about being sick," say, "I am

interested in what I can do to take care of my health."

Instead of "I am *anxious* about my new job," say, "I am *excited* to begin my new job."

Instead of "This person is so *difficult* to deal with," say, "I have been dealing with a very *challenging* person lately."

Instead of "Thank God, we *survived* the ordeal," say, "With God's help, we *overcame* the obstacles."

Instead of "I'll *try* to quit smoking," say, "I'll *do* it!"

One of the most challenging things to train in life is our tongue, yet our choice of words has a powerful effect on us. Scientific research has shown that different words trigger different brain chemicals, resulting in shifts toward either more positive or more negative life experiences. Our words, in other words, can fundamentally affect our mental, physical, and spiritual well-being, which in turn affects everyone around us. That's why we want to watch what we say. We need to make sure that our vocabulary is one that enhances life and contributes to respect.

Chapter Seven

Trust

Trust in the LORD with all your heart
and lean not on your own understanding;
in all your ways acknowledge him,
and he will make your paths straight.

PROVERBS 3:5

We are now ready to clear the last hurdle standing between us and love. If we lack trust, we are unable to love and be loved, but before we can trust others, we must learn to trust ourselves. We do that by understanding what triggers our emotions and by practicing the thoughts, words, and actions associated with honesty, integrity, and respect. For many of us, this is not an easy thing to do.

> *As soon as you trust yourself, you will know how to live.*
>
> —GOETHE

TURNING NOTHING INTO SOMETHING

When I was thirty-one, I married a very bright and interesting man with myriad gifts. A sculptor, painter, and experienced seaman, Mark had unique insight into people and life. Being married to him provided me with many one-of-a-kind opportunities and adventures.

I learned to read navigational charts and electronic equipment and lived on a thirty-six-foot fishing vessel for eighteen months, fishing for shrimp. I was one of four crewmembers who helped skipper an eighty-foot salmon tender through the inside passage of southeast Alaska. Since Mark was gone for months at a time and I was far from family and friends, I became involved in rescue work in the Aleutian Chain, received Alaska state certification in Firefighting and Emergency Medicine Class II, and worked as a corrections officer for the Dutch Harbor/Unalaska Public Safety Department. I also taught chorus for college credit and worked as a volunteer counselor with an alcohol rehabilitation program. In the beginning, I found all of this tremendously exciting.

When the excitement wore off, however, I felt increasingly isolated. As lonely as I was when Mark was gone, I felt even lonelier when I was with him. Although he was highly intelligent, he had been brought up in a very poor family and had only a sixth-grade education. As a result, he had a negative self-image that manifested itself as a deep disgust for people who were educated or financially successful. We *never* socialized with people who had a college education.

During the eleven years we were married, Mark paid no taxes, and creditors chased us constantly. We never had a permanent residence. We were either living on our boat, staying at his mother's house, house-sitting, or renting a room somewhere. We lived in a small apartment twice, but only for a short period each time.

Mark lacked self-control, and when his temper flared at home, he would sweep a shelf clean of whatever was on it, books, statues—even the stereo and speakers. Once he bashed my guitar to bits because I didn't want him to whittle down the width of the neck. When his temper flared during fishing season, he would jump aboard another vessel and grab the "offending" skipper by the neck, slam him against the bulkhead, and punch him. He never hit me, but I lived in constant fear that someday he would.

Why did I remain in that relationship? For one thing, Mark was very nurturing to me when I was sick. My illness was one way I got attention from him, and caring for me was one way he controlled me. Looking back, I know that he did nothing that I didn't somehow allow. We were both in it together. I felt like a nothing; he felt like a nothing. Our marriage was a rich environment to experience nothing, but it had absolutely nothing to do with love. Yet I remember preferring to die rather than leave. At that time, I would have endured anything in order not to live life alone. *Why?* Because I did not trust myself.

I told no one about my unhappiness and fear of Mark. In fact, I usually spoke of our relationship as a healthy and happy one. After I divorced, a longtime friend said to me, "Shelley, do you realize how differently you behaved when Mark was in town and when he wasn't?"

"What do you mean?" I asked.

"When Mark was with you, you kept very quiet, and your head was downcast most of the time. Your normal high energy and enthusiasm for this community simply faded away when he was around. Even though you never said anything about problems in your marriage, I felt something was very wrong with that relationship."

My behavior had told my friend that I was not being honest.

Before I could learn to trust myself, I had to admit that my dependency was the only thing keeping me in that relationship. Deep inside, I knew that God's plan for my life was for me to make something of the gifts He had given me and to become something worthy of returning to Him. If I wanted to *feel* like something instead of nothing, I had to *behave* that way. I had to step out, trusting that God would keep me on the right path. Knowing that He had a purpose for my life was what enabled me to trust myself.

What loneliness is more lonely than mistrust?

—GEORGE ELIOT

WHAT'S LOVE GOT TO DO WITH IT?

If you want to see how trust impacts relationships, watch pets interact with their owners. You'll find that some animals are very trusting and loving, while others are skittish or mean. If an animal doesn't show spontaneous affection for his master, or cowers when his master raises his voice, he is demonstrating a lack of trust. Just because an animal stays around doesn't necessarily mean he trusts or loves his owner. The owner provides food and shelter, and an animal will stay for that, even when abused.

People can act the same way. Sometimes they remain in an abusive environment because on some level they believe they get something from it. Unlike animals, however, people have the power to rationalize their experiences. I saw this when I volunteered as a group leader for the national organization Womenspace.

Once a week I met with women who were in abusive and even life-threatening relationships. Over and over I heard: "I can't be without him"; "I still love him even though he hurts me"; "Deep down he is really a good person"; "He doesn't really mean to hurt me"; "I know he loves me." These women had remained with their partners under the constant threat of physical, psychological, or sexual abuse, and yet they believed their partners' behavior had something to do with love.

If you tell yourself things like this, you'll act on what you wish were true, not on what you really know to be true. When you're being honest, you know what motivates you. Trust is having the courage to act upon the inner wisdom God has implanted in your heart.

TRUST IS LEARNED AND EARNED

In part, my desire to help women in abusive relationships stemmed from my own experience seventeen years earlier. I related to their feelings of helplessness and confusion, but I also knew that they bore some of the responsibility for the lethal games they were playing with their partners.

We talked about the destructive behaviors. We talked about what was missing from their relationships; what it was they thought they had; and what they, intentionally or unintentionally, contributed to that relationship. When I asked them what finally made them flee, they said, "Because I can't trust him anymore" or "He doesn't trust me at all."

The common denominator of all these relationships was a lack of honesty, integrity, and respect. Only when these women were able to identify their motives, admit their share of responsibility for their situation, and honestly accept the necessity for change in themselves and in their partners were they able to evaluate the possibilities for reconciliation. The transformation of these courageous women created a powerful and lasting impression on me—one that planted the seed of the life-enhancing concepts I am sharing with you now.

When we live in an environment where there is no trust, we are constantly on guard and stressed, incapable of experiencing love. By freeing ourselves from irrational fears and rationalizations and by practicing honesty, integrity, and respect, we engender trust—first in ourselves and then in others. As trust increases, so does the ability to love and be loved.

A man who doesn't trust himself can never truly trust anyone else.

—CARDINAL DE RETZ

Chapter Eight

Love

God is love.
Whoever lives in love
lives in God,
and God in him.

1 JOHN 4:16

Looking again at the left hand graphic, we can see that once we clear the hurdle of trust, we *slide* into the cradle of love. We often think that we strive for love, but what we really work toward is trust. Love is a natural feeling, waiting and wanting to happen. But like all feelings, it is the result of how we act. We experience it by giving and receiving in a way that enhances both our lives and the lives of others.

Love is the gift of behaving to enhance life.

—CLAY STARLIN

ACTS OF LOVE

After my neck surgery, my doctors recommended that I stay away from Foxfire while I was healing, so I didn't go see him for a month. When at last I arrived at the barn for a visit, Foxy was grazing at the far end of the pasture. I whistled and raised my arm. He raised his head, nickered loudly, and then galloped across the pasture, his tail and mane flying in the wind.

As soon as he reached the gate, Foxy suddenly stopped and began to gently sniff around my brace. Soon he started to lick my head and face. He knew something was up—and I knew he knew. Right then I decided I had to make every effort to go to the annual Memorial Day weekend horse camp outing at Fort Rock with my old friends from the Lane County Mounted Sheriff's Posse.

I asked Ken to help me pack for the outing. He did, but he also reminded me that it would take place just eight days after my surgery for cancer. How would I feel? I persisted. I knew that whatever healing I needed would be enhanced by spending time in the fresh air of the desert with my husband, my horse, and the friends who had taught me so much about riding.

We finished packing just hours before we drove to Portland for the operation. After the surgery, I discovered that the lower right side of my face and my right shoulder muscles were paralyzed. I could hardly move my right arm. The surgeon assured me that with physical therapy and time, I could overcome this unexpected challenge.

Meanwhile, my desire to make the desert outing increased, even though I knew it would place a tremendous burden on Ken. He would have to do all the setting up, cooking, and cleanup for us. He would have to feed, groom, and saddle Foxy, and he would have to assist me into the saddle and trust, as I rode away from him, that I would be safe on the trail.

Eight days after my surgery, without a single discouraging word, Ken packed the Explorer, loaded Foxy into the horse trailer, and headed for Fort Rock. He did everything with such love. For the first three nights, while the posse looked after Foxy, he drove me home so I could shower and get a more comfortable night's sleep. By the fourth night, I was doing so well that we slept in our tent.

On the first day I could ride for only an hour, and I kept my right arm in a sling. Foxy, who usually jitterbugged down the trail, was unusually quiet—even when other horses cantered past him. Each day I increased the amount of time I rode and decreased the time I kept my arm in the sling. Soon I was riding four to five hours a day and even doing some trotting.

Much to my amazement and gratitude, I found that by the end of the trip I didn't need physical therapy or pain medication. Ken's love had manifested itself in his willingness to spend quality time with me and to perform selfless acts of service; Foxy had shown his love the only way he knew how—through physical contact. Their loving behavior had not only enhanced my life, but also accelerated my healing.

> *There is a land of the living and a land of the dead and the bridge is love.*
>
> — THORNTON WILDER

WORDS OF LOVE

If I hadn't already learned the importance of loving myself, I might never have had that healing experience. I might have considered myself unworthy of the acts of love needed to make the outing possible and just stayed home. But if we reject ourselves like that, we cannot receive love from others—no matter how much we might crave it.

One of the ways that people express love is through words of affirmation, yet for years I had trouble accepting a compliment. I would always fend it off by coming up with a list of reasons why I didn't deserve it. A very kind eighty-five-year-old woman helped me break that bad habit.

One day after I sang two classical vocal solos at a beautiful memorial service, that charming, refined lady walked over to me and complimented me on my performance. Although I had trained as a classical musician, I had never felt particularly comfortable with that performance style, so I responded to her praise with a litany of reasons why I hadn't done better.

Taking my hand in hers, she said, "My dear, so as not to diminish the joy I receive in sharing my appreciation of your singing, a simple 'thank you' would do. If 'thank you' is too difficult, or if you feel you cannot take personal credit for your talent, perhaps you might reply, 'I am pleased you enjoyed it.' In that way, you'll not diminish yourself, the talent God gave you, or the person who feels moved to express feelings of appreciation for you."

In order to love others, we must have a healthy perspective on self-love. In denigrating myself, I was not behaving in a way that enhanced that caring woman's life because I was not behaving in a way that enhanced my own.

This particular incident had to do with using words to express love, but the language of love goes far beyond the words we use. Another part of the language of love is giving and receiving gifts. People may tune out what we say, but they can't miss our behavior.

GIFTS OF LOVE

When we think about giving people gifts of love, we usually think about the giving part, not the receiving part. I learned a memorable lesson about giving and receiving from a client I worked with in weekly therapy sessions for six months.

In our first session, Roger described himself as having felt dead to love for most of his adult years. Diagnosed with clinical depression, he agreed to begin medication and to remain in therapy until he saw a positive change. Adept at working through the self-evaluation process, he learned how to give lovingly to others, and by the end of therapy he was reaping the benefits of his new behavior.

Two months later, he returned. He had begun dating Allison and had grown very fond of her. He hoped their relationship would result in marriage. However, there was a serious problem. Although he had learned how to give, he had not yet learned how to receive. When Allison tried to give him gifts to express her appreciation for him, he could not receive them graciously. As a result, she felt rejected, and soon they began drifting apart. "You don't seem to like or appreciate what I try to do for you," she told him.

Roger told me that he knew Allison loved him. The problem was that although he could easily accept her love, he felt undeserving of her loving attention.

"Why do you give her gifts?" I asked him.

"Because I care a great deal for her," he said. "And I feel really good when I see how much she appreciates it."

Then I asked, "Do you think that most of us want to love and be loved?"

"Yes."

"Do you want to deny the people you care about the opportunity to feel good in the same way you do?"

He shook his head. "Of course I don't," he said.

"Then the next time someone wants to give you a gift, remember how good it makes you feel when you give to others, and choose to accept it."

"I hadn't thought of it in that way before," he said.

Choosing to receive love is just as important as choosing to give it. We must learn to love ourselves and to graciously give and receive love. As we do, we will begin to experience both exhilaration and inner peace— sure signs that that we are living in love. And when we are living in *love*, we are living in *God*.

Love does not die easily…. It thrives in the face of all life's hazards, save one—neglect.

—JAMES D. BRYDEN

Part Three

Staying on Track

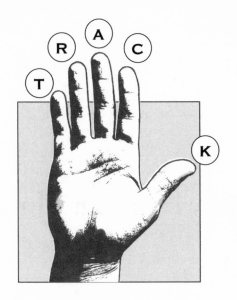

Chapter Nine

Truth

*"You will know the truth,
and the truth will set you free."*

JOHN 8:32

The morning after Jesus was arrested in the Garden of Gethsemane, He was taken to the palace of Pontius Pilate. In the course of answering the Roman governor's questions, Jesus said, "Everyone on the side of truth listens to me." Pilate's rhetorical reply, "What is truth?" has echoed down through the centuries.

Many people believe there is no such thing as truth, so they don't even try to find it. Yet I believe that we must discover it, for knowing the truth can free us from destructive thinking and behaviors. In my own life, the discovery of truth set me on the path to healing and emotional maturity.

*The truth that makes men free is for the most part
the truth which men prefer not to hear.*

—HERBERT AGAR

SET FREE

I was almost forty years old when I completed a post-graduate program as a physician's assistant in family medicine. Although I had graduated and passed national board exams, I considered these accomplishments flukes, and the thought of venturing into the world to practice medicine terrified me.

As soon as I started my first job, the autoimmune disorder I had had since childhood (eosinophilic gastroenteritis) flared up. After I ate, my skin broke out in hives, my head pounded, and I had severe abdominal cramping followed by projectile vomiting. I developed eczema, asthma, and a number of sensitivities to food and the environment. Six months later, my weight had plummeted from my normal 125 pounds to 85, and my hair was falling out. I no longer had the physical strength or stamina to walk on my own.

When my dear friend from childhood, Debbie Newman, learned about the state of my health, she flew me to her home in Southern California. Debbie and her husband, Terry, supported me with prayer while they researched medical solutions and drove me to every innovative, thorough physician they could find. No one knew what to do. Physicians at Jewish Hospital, a Denver facility specializing in allergies, told Terry that I was too ill and vulnerable to be safe from devastating infections if I were hospitalized. Instead, I began an alternative and highly controversial therapy intended to desensitize me to allergens. The medication brought some relief, yet I continued to weaken.

Then one day Debbie heard about a Christian counselor who practiced prayer and regression techniques in order to identify mind-body connections that could be contributing to poor health. When Debbie told me about Bonnie's methods, I felt uneasy. What were her credentials? Would she wave a plucked chicken over my head or perform a frenzied dance while chanting bizarre incantations? I didn't reveal my fears, for at that point I thought any intervention would be worth a try. I agreed to see Bonnie—once.

On the day of my appointment, I was carried into Bonnie's home and placed on her couch. She asked me to tell her "my story." After I did, she said, "Clearly, you've had some unpleasant experiences. Yet although you have accomplished many things, you still see yourself in a negative way. Do you consider yourself a failure or a success in life?"

I sat staring at her for a long time, feeling my anger rise. Finally I said, "Isn't it rather obvious that I demonstrate a profound failure to thrive?"

"Yes," she said. "However, you didn't answer my question. Do you consider yourself a failure or a success in life?"

I was barely able to control my anger. "A failure," I replied.

"You know, my impression of you is that you are an incredible success."

I felt my throat constrict. "God, just get me out of here!" I mumbled. Then I shut down. I had no intention of uttering another word.

Bonnie persisted. "Possibly you don't understand what I observe in you?"

I said nothing and averted my eyes.

"Shelley, wouldn't you agree that your negative perceptions of yourself are based on some experiences that were out of your control?"

I looked up.

"Although you have achieved worthy goals, you have never accepted the credit in a positive way."

I kept looking at her.

"Don't you see what an incredible *success* you have been in believing your negative thoughts? Your illness is in part due to your impaired belief system. It has created a powerful and negative physical response, and your body screams the results. Can you imagine what your life could be like if you were to put just one quarter of that negative thinking energy into positive and constructive thoughts?"

All of the sudden I got it! I was dumbfounded at the truth of what she had uncovered: My own negative thoughts were perpetuating my unhappiness and preventing me from getting well.

I came to understand that I had been hoping that nothing would be found to improve my health. At the time I finished my medical training, my mother had just died, and I was becoming increasingly aware of how unhealthy my first marriage was. I did not *want* to continue life with my husband, and I did not believe I *could* continue life without my mother's emotional support. Deep inside, I had decided that dying was easier than facing my circumstances.

It is a tragedy how often people choose a physical or psychological death over discovering the truth that sets them free to live. Bonnie had done me a great service in helping me acknowledge the truth about myself.

The unexamined life is not worth living.

— PLATO

A SELF-FULFILLING PROPHECY

One day an angry, distraught woman came to my office. She told me she had already seen several other therapists, but they hadn't helped her. She said they didn't understand her unique life circumstances, didn't listen to her, and didn't give her the support she believed a therapist should provide. All of them, she said, asked her to learn to do things she felt incapable of doing. "But I've heard so many good things about you," she continued. "I'm convinced *you* will help me. No one else will."

Sandra's circumstances *were* unique. She had a hereditary form of macular degeneration, and she did in fact need help to accomplish many tasks. The problem was that she played up her helplessness and used it as a way to control people. Over time she had come to expect others to meet all her needs. But by the time she was forty, her dishonest manipulation was causing her husband, children, and friends to pull away from her. Understandably frightened, she sought support in therapy.

During our early sessions, I listened, validated her feelings, and at appropriate times challenged her to examine her role as victim. We discussed the consequences of continuing that behavior as well as the benefits of choosing to take more responsibility for her life. But each time we got close to the truth that would lead her into a healthier future, she either changed the subject or found countless reasons why none of my suggestions would work.

> *"What is truth," said jesting Pilate;*
> *and would not stay for an answer.*
>
> —FRANCIS BACON

After several weeks it became clear to me that Sandra was not willing to know the truth about the part she played in her deteriorating relationships. Like the therapists before me, I was holding up a mirror to her, but she was not willing to look in it. She believed that as long as she could convince her husband that she was incapable of doing more, his guilt over leaving her helpless would keep him from leaving her. In her eyes, I was rapidly becoming just another therapist who didn't understand her, and eventually the day came when I felt we had to discontinue the sessions.

"Sandra," I said, "this is very difficult for me. However, I realize that although I have done my best to help you, I am at a loss to know what else I can do."

She stared at me for some time. Then she put her head down and said nothing for a few minutes. When she looked back up, she said, "You people all say the same things to me. But if I become more independent and take more responsibility for my life, my husband *will* leave me. My kids *will* stop taking care of me. I am over fifty years old. Why would I want to do that at this time in my life?"

I had no answer. Sandra did not want to know the truth, and so she clung to the very behaviors that were destroying her relationships. In the absence of truth, her behavior turned her fears into a self-fulfilling prophecy.

Once we become willing to find out and act upon the truth about ourselves, we are prepared to become mature adults who take responsibility for our lives.

Chapter Ten

Responsibility

Each of us will give an
account of himself to God.

ROMANS 14:12

Taking responsibility basically means holding ourselves accountable to someone. Responsibility and trust are closely related. Others show us that they trust us by giving us responsibilities; we take responsibility when we are willing to answer to them for what they have entrusted to us. In essence, a responsibility is a temporary gift that we are to make wise use of while it is ours. Wherever there is this gift, there is a responsibility.

Behaving responsibly keeps us on track to becoming mature and loving adults. When we take responsibility for what we have received, our behavior demonstrates love not only to the one who gave it, but also to those who are affected by it.

> *The more freedom we enjoy, the greater the responsibility*
> *we bear, toward others as well as ourselves.*
>
> —OSCAR ARIAS SÁNCHEZ

A LESSON IN RESPONSIBILITY

When I was nearly four years old, my family attended a special Christmas service at a large church in Los Angeles. The choir sat in a balcony above the congregation, hidden from view. As soon as they began singing, a wonderful sensation came over me. It was my first experience with total body gooseflesh. Never had I heard such beautiful sounds! I looked all around, trying to figure out where they were coming from. Seeing nothing, I gently nudged my mother and whispered, "Mama, are we in heaven?" At that moment I discovered my first gift from God, and from that day forward music became a way for me to give something to the world.

When I was ten years old, I auditioned for the children's choir at our church. After I was accepted, I committed myself to attend the regular rehearsal and performance schedules. Singing with that group was both exciting and rewarding. We learned a large repertoire of many beautiful songs of praise to God, which we sang in four-part harmony. Later on I was encouraged to audition for solo parts, and eventually I became a regular in the program. I *was* in heaven!

At about twelve or thirteen years old, I was still singing in the choir, but I was starting to feel a bit restless and lazy. Learning the music seemed easy enough and, besides, during the rehearsal time my friends were hanging out at the plaza fountain downtown. I decided not to go to the weekly rehearsals so I could be with my friends. On the day my plan was to go into action, I casually informed my mother of my decision.

"Well, Shelley," she said, "you certainly don't have to go to rehearsals. You're free to choose. But if you don't go, you'll have to drop out of choir."

"What do you mean?" I asked. "I can still sing with them. I learn the music really fast. It isn't necessary for me to be at every rehearsal. They wouldn't even miss me."

She sat me down. "Honey," she said. "This is not about you or how well you think you're doing. Committing yourself to any project that includes others means that people are counting on you, whether you think so or not. What do you think would happen if everyone in your group behaved in this way?"

My mother's gentle but firm admonition has stuck with me all these years. It has caused me to think carefully before I join any group. If I cannot follow through on a commitment, I do not make it.

Your talents are gifts from God. When He gave you life, He also gave you the gift of choosing what you will make of them. With freedom of choice comes responsibility. Taking responsibility in this area means identifying your thoughts, deciding what you want, and exchanging self-defeating behaviors for ones that enhance your life. Ultimately, your choices will determine what kind of gift your life will be when you hand it back to God.

> *What is a person responsible for?*
> *Everything he thinks, says, or does. Why?*
> *Because no matter what or whom one can blame for the*
> *circumstances of his life, he is still stuck with the*
> *consequences of everything he thinks, says, or does.*
>
> —SIDNEY MADWED

A LIFE OF CHOICE

When Ken began complaining about his life a few years ago, I knew something was wrong. Normally when he's faced with a challenge, he gives the situation considerable thought and then moves toward a solution without verbalizing his complaints. This time, however, his complaining began to put pressure on our relationship.

Over and over, Ken complained of his unhappiness and the growing fatigue he felt as a result of our new medical practice. It was a small, private family clinic. We had committed to building a new facility and were beginning our practice with all new patients. As responsible employers, our financial obligations for the business and to our employees came first, but the HMOs were making deep cuts in payments for patient services, while the state-subsidized insurance plan reimbursed at minimum levels. For two and a half years, Ken had worked four twelve-hour shifts during the week, as well as every weekend, yet he earned less than half the salary he could have commanded in a larger group practice.

Two days after the new clinic opened, my colon ruptured, and I could not practice for several months. Six months later, Ken suffered two small strokes, but he continued working in order to keep the clinic open and our employees paid. Thanks to his healthy lifestyle and many loving prayers, he fully recovered from the strokes. But his joy for life evaporated.

I tried to respond to Ken's frequent complaints in positive and respectful ways. I validated his concerns and encouraged him to move forward. However, he remained stuck. He had practiced medicine for more than thirty years. Now approaching his sixty-first birthday, he had no other means of making a living. Unable to envision a way out of his dilemma, he shut down to suggestions and fell deeper into discouragement. My own sorrow and frustration grew.

Usually, we addressed the events of our lives while relaxing in our hot tub, a place where we felt free to speak openly. However, one rainy night while we were soaking, Ken began complaining again, and my patience reached its limit. No one could have been more surprised than I was when I heard myself say, "Honey, maybe you should just suck it up or get a life."

Ken stared at me in wide-eyed silence.

What have I done? I asked myself.

Gently, I pressed on. "Ken, if you were to leave medicine, what would you like to do?"

He remained silent for some time. I waited. He still didn't speak. I still waited. Finally he said softly, "Maybe I could be a janitor. I get a lot of satisfaction from organizing and keeping things clean."

"Is there anything else about being a janitor that appeals to you?" I asked.

He answered immediately. "Yes, I would have some relief from the constant demands of being responsible for the health and lives of my patients."

"Okay, Ken," I said. "If that's how you really feel, go

for it. If that will renew your joy, do whatever it takes. I support you 100 percent!"

After a moment, Ken continued. "That may not provide sufficient means to meet our current financial obligations," he said. "Maybe I could get into some kind of construction. I have always enjoyed making things, but over the last several years I haven't had the opportunity. I could take some classes at the community college. I could call Richard and see what he's up to." Richard had designed and built our beautiful cedar home in the hills of Eugene.

Little did I know how my brazen words would affect our lives. Shortly after our conversation in the hot tub, Ken called Richard. Then he enrolled in a home maintenance and repair class at our local community college. Within a year, we sold our home in Eugene and moved to Bend, where with a partner we built an award-winning model spec home.

Was this radical change in lifestyle easy? *No.* In fact, it was very challenging. Has it been worth it? *Yes!* Once Ken accepted the truth about himself, made choices, and courageously followed through, his health improved. He no longer has type 2 diabetes, and his cholesterol level and blood pressure are now in the healthy range.

Just as important, when he was willing to accept responsibility for God's gift of life, he naturally developed a healthier attitude, and his joy returned. He is now involved with VIM (Volunteers in Medicine), which is building a clinic where volunteers will serve people unable to pay for medical care. Ken is actually excited about practicing medicine again!

To decide, to be at the level of choice,
is to take responsibility for your life
and to be in control of your life.

—ABBIE DALE

Chapter Eleven

Attitude

Your attitude should be the same as that of Christ Jesus:
Who, being in very nature God...
made himself nothing,
taking the very nature of a servant.

PHILIPPIANS 2:5–7

During the past fifteen years, the relatively new field of psychoneuroimmunology (PSI) has revealed how our state of mind releases chemicals that affect our brain chemistry and immune systems. It works the other way, too. When challenged or enhanced, our immune systems influence our brain chemistry and thus our states of mind. This means that the attitudes we bring to all the circumstances of our lives can determine not only if we thrive, but even if we survive.

Victor Frankl, an eminent psychiatrist, was imprisoned in Auschwitz and other concentration camps for three years during WWII. From his experiences, Frankl concluded that it did not really matter what he and his fellow prisoners expected from life, but rather what life expected from them. Once we know what that is, it's up to us to adjust our attitude accordingly.

> *The last of the human freedoms—*
> *to choose one's attitude in any given set of circumstances,*
> *to choose one's own way.*
>
> —VICTOR FRANKL

LET THE STRONG SAY, "I AM WEAK."

Since God is the giver of life, I equate knowing what life expects from me with knowing His will for my life. For me, that's easier said than done, so recently I worked my way through a course on how to know and do God's will. Every once in a while the author threw in a question, and I must admit that I wasn't confident about a lot of my answers. But finally I came across one I was sure about. The question was: "What is a servant?" *Piece of cake,* I thought.

When I was young, Brownies and Girl Scouts had taught me the value and joy of serving others, and I carried that attitude into adulthood. I have always volunteered to serve and have done so with a glad and willing heart. So I picked up my pen and confidently wrote, "A good servant is a person who joyfully serves the needs of others." Eager to earn an "A" for my good answer, I flipped the page to find out what the author had to say.

It was a humbling experience. In the first place, the author suggested that if we tried to serve others in our own strength, we were on the wrong track. He took it for granted that we wouldn't even attempt to serve others until we found out what God wanted us to do. True servants go to Him first. That way, He can make us what we need to be to accomplish His purposes. I hadn't even mentioned God!

A light went on in my head. Pleasing others can be either a self-serving or a selfless way of life. I realized that my motive for serving had been mainly to please other people in ways that would reward my ego, and I knew it was time for an attitude adjustment. A great attitude is the result of focusing on something great—and there is nothing greater than God. My attitude now is that I truly serve others only when I allow Him to lead me to those He intends for me to serve. When we bring our attitude into line with God's plan for our life, our service has the power to help redeem shattered lives and spirits.

> *A great attitude does much more than turn*
> *on the lights in our worlds; it seems to magically*
> *connect us to all sorts of serendipitous opportunities*
> *that were somehow absent before the change.*
>
> —EARL NIGHTINGALE

LET THE WEAK SAY, "I AM STRONG."

In 1996, Karen came to see me with her eight-year-old daughter, Jennifer. The little girl was confined to a wheelchair, and the crippling effects of her advancing juvenile rheumatoid arthritis were alarming. Her limbs were misshapen and appeared painful to move, and her beautiful little face was swollen out of proportion to the rest of her body from the long-term effects of prednisone use.

Greatly distraught, Karen expressed her deep concern about Jennifer's condition and her future. "What will become of my daughter?" she asked. "It's so frightening to think how painful it will be for her to get around in the world. What is Jennifer supposed to say? How is she supposed to react to closed and cruel minds?"

With her eyes averted from her mother and me, Jennifer sat motionless and speechless. When Karen began weeping uncontrollably, Jennifer gripped the arms of her wheelchair, her gaze riveted on the floor. Though I could find no appropriate means to soothe Jennifer, my spirit reached out to hers. Sensing my attention, she looked up, and our eyes and hearts met for the first time. Her gaze seemed to reveal deep understanding and compassion for her mother.

Karen came to the second session alone, and as we talked about Jennifer's challenges, I learned that she loved music and was gifted with a beautiful singing voice. Karen had the same gift, but she had always kept it hidden from others because she felt too vulnerable to stand in front of an audience. Childhood sexual abuse had thwarted her ability to feel safe and accepted, and unwittingly, she was teaching this attitude to her daughter. Could Jennifer, physically vulnerable, survive in the world her mother found so threatening?

Karen's tortured demeanor revealed the strong and negative belief system that had kept her fearfully locked inside herself for many years. "This is so unfair," she sobbed. "Jennifer doesn't deserve this. What can I possibly do to ensure that she will have the opportunity for a better life?"

"You can change your attitude and behavior, " I said. "If you want to help your daughter, you must first demonstrate a healthy and positive attitude around her. Based on your attitude and actions, Jennifer will view life's opportunities as goals that are either possible or impossible for her to achieve."

Karen did not return to therapy for nearly a year. Years later she confessed that my calm response had deeply angered her. Though my message stung, it also produced an irritation that festered until it led to a change in Karen's attitude and resulted in positive action.

Six years later, Karen became a successful advocate for Jennifer, as well as for her profoundly dyslexic and musically gifted son, Robert, whose teachers had refused to move him on to the next grade, provide special tutelage, or even acknowledge that he was highly intelligent. Because the school system would not provide wheelchair access to the stage, Jennifer could not perform with her classmates. Relentlessly, Karen sought more acceptable educational, physical, and psychological solutions for her two children and others like them—children with extreme learning challenges and special education needs. Because of her persistence, her school system now provides wheelchair access to the theater and special programs for learning-challenged children.

Today, Karen sings in church and community musical productions with her children and husband. Jennifer, still in her wheelchair, was recently given the role of Little Cossette in the musical *Les Miserables*, a part she shared on alternating nights with another student at her school. Robert was awarded a musical scholarship to the University of Oregon.

By changing her attitude, Karen not only gained reentry to the world from which she had locked herself out, but also created a new world for those she loved. She altered an entire local educational system and forever enhanced the lives of those who were fortunate enough to sail on the sea of her powerful attitude change.

A shift of purpose is at the heart of any change in attitude. As we shift our purpose and adjust our attitude, we find ourselves developing character.

> *Could we change our attitude,*
> *we should not only see life differently,*
> *but life itself would come to be different.*
> —KATHERINE MANSFIELD

Chapter Twelve

Character

*"Do to others as you would
have them do to you."*

LUKE 6:31

To help us develop character, God has written the Golden Rule on the tablets of our hearts. The moment something happens that annoys, affronts, or afflicts us, we somehow *know* that under similar circumstances the same thing would annoy, afflict, or affront all other people. Our consciousness of that truth equips us to do to others as we would have them do to us.

While awareness of the Golden Rule is innate, character is not. It develops amid the temptations and trials of life as we choose to incline our heart away from self and toward God and others.

> *You cannot dream yourself into a character;*
> *you must hammer and forge yourself one.*
>
> —JAMES A. FROUDE

THE FIRST HALF OF THE EQUATION

At the age of two, I manifested symptoms of severe allergic reactions to foods and the environment. Asthma, fatigue, hay fever, and eczema were the most obvious. Yellow-crusted and oozing-red lesions covered my body. During the worst outbreaks, I slept with plastic sheeting and pillowcases to prevent my face and body from sticking to them. At night I wore large cuffs on my arms so that I couldn't bend them to scratch.

I was to be enrolled in kindergarten when I was four and a half, so when I was between three and four years of age, my mother consulted a psychologist. She expected negative, if innocent, responses to my appearance and wanted to learn how she could help me handle the fearful and repulsed reactions of others when they first saw me. Advised to deemphasize emotional responses, my mother educated me about my condition and taught me to respond calmly when others overreacted.

We lived in Southern California, where temperatures are high in September, and on the first day of kindergarten I wore a cotton short-sleeved dress. My mother held my hand as we walked to my classroom. Many eager children were waiting outside with their mothers. As we approached the group, curious children and mothers turned toward us. I remember a sudden quiet and eyes staring at me. I remember a voice that said "Ouuuu... what's that? What's wrong with her, Mommy?" Placing my hands on my hips, I faced them and said, "It's eggs-e-ma, don'tcha know?"

I received similar comments and reactions from some of my teachers and peers throughout my school years. Depending on my age and the situation, these responses annoyed, affronted, or afflicted me. At a very early age I knew the effects the actions of others had on my life, and I knew how I wanted others to treat me. I had yet to learn the other half of the character equation, but with my mother's help, I did.

THE CURE FOR A SELFISH HEART

One day when I was young, my mother overheard my best friend and me criticizing other friends. Hearing our cruel laughter and recognizing our mean-spiritedness, she told us this story:

Once upon a time, a young child was given an entire closet filled with new and wonderful toys of all kinds, shapes, colors, and sizes. The child was told, "You may keep all these toys. All you have to do is take care of them."

Selecting toys from the shelves to play with, the child realized that each one had some flaw. Some were boring. One had a missing piece. Another had an undesirable color. A few had torn clothing or thinning hair. So the child began throwing away all the toys that had "something wrong" with them.

One day when the child went to the closet to play, no more toys were left. Sad, and then angry, the child threw a tantrum and demanded more toys.

"When you throw away toys simply because they are imperfect or old," the child was lovingly told, "someday all your toys will be gone."

Sow a thought, you reap an act;
Sow an act, you reap a habit;
Sow a habit, you reap a character;
Sow a character, you reap a destiny.

—EUGENE P. BERTIN

To live by the Golden Rule, we need to be able to picture ourselves in another person's place. Character is what enables us to imagine ourselves as an imperfect toy on someone else's shelf. It allows us to appreciate all people for who they are and to treat them as we would like them to treat us. It is the key to loving others as we love ourselves.

THE BEAT GOES ON

Character is not forged in isolation, and it is not formed overnight. Throughout our lives we will find ourselves in situations that will call out either the best or the worst in us. We know we are developing character when the best comes out despite our circumstances.

I grew up as an outsider in an affluent, close-knit community. I didn't come from a wealthy family like most of my classmates did, and I wasn't pretty or popular. In fact, I was considered a geek. And, of course, I had "eggs-e-ma, don'tcha know." My face, legs, and arms were still unsightly, and the medications I took for asthma made me overexcited and talkative. It really was quite understandable why most kids didn't want to hang out with me—but I still wanted them to.

One day, when I was in eighth grade, my family had supper with friends, and as soon as we finished eating, the four of us kids ran outside to play cops and robbers.

My brother, Michael, and John were the robbers, and Karen and I were the cops. Karen and I scoured the neighborhood for the criminals, and eventually I found Michael hiding in some dense foliage. He took off like a gazelle, and I followed in gleeful pursuit.

Shortness of breath halted me momentarily, and Michael dashed away. Once I caught my breath, I thought I could foil his escape by taking a shortcut through our friends' dining room. The sliding glass doors were so clean that I thought they were open, and I ran full steam ahead. The next thing I knew, I was lying on the floor amidst glass shards in a pool of my own blood.

Three hours and seventy-six stitches later, our family doctor had sutured my right leg, right arm, and face. A week later, I returned to class with a white crisscross bandage over my upper lip and nose. When the bandage was removed the following week, there was a bright red scar stretching from under my left nostril to the top corner of my right upper lip. It would take a long time for the redness to fade. As far as my classmates were concerned, it was another humiliation, but I was able to treat the incident with humor, as my mother had taught me.

That September, when my classmates and I began ninth grade, we were bused twenty miles to a new school. It was scary for everyone. We would have to establish ourselves in new surroundings with new teachers and kids protecting their home turf. As intimidating as this was, I saw the change as an opportunity. Since we were all in the same boat, I hoped my classmates would be more inclined to accept me as one of the group. I hoped they would somehow need me as much as I needed them.

Soon after we cleared the bus lane, a group of the most popular kids huddled. Hearing their laughter, I cautiously approached them. None of them noticed. I was just about to speak when I heard one of the girls say, "And besides that, she talks too much and her skin always looks so icky." More laughter.

An odd thing happened. When I was younger, perhaps because of the way my mother had taught me to handle insensitive remarks, the rejections I encountered had never registered as strongly as they did on this day. Now I felt pierced through and through. My gut wrenched with pain and discouragement.

But then something wonderful took over my heart. I stepped back and said to myself, *Dear God, please help me to always remember what this feels like. I never want to treat people unkindly just because they look or act different than me.* It was a revelation. In the midst of humiliation and rejection, I was able to choose to incline my heart away from self and toward God and others.

I was becoming a person of character.

Chapter Thirteen

Knowledge

We demolish arguments and every pretension
that sets itself up against the knowledge of God,
and we take captive every thought to make it obedient to Christ.

2 CORINTHIANS 10:5

Knowledge gives us the capacity to choose healthy behaviors. Adding to our knowledge of how our minds, bodies, and spirits work enables us to treat ourselves in life-enhancing ways. We know that we nurture our minds when we develop artistic skills, engage in stimulating conversations, or study topics of interest. We know that we nurture our bodies when we exercise, rest, and avoid toxic substances. We know that we nurture our spirits when we meditate, listen to uplifting music, or read inspirational literature.

Yet I believe that the greatest knowledge we can aspire to is to know God, for that is what enables us to understand His unique purpose for our lives. There are several ways *to know about* God—seeing His handiwork in nature and studying His Word—but there is only one way *to know* God, and that is through a personal relationship with Him. When we have that relationship, we enter His kingdom—a realm where miracles happen.

> *No man can know himself as he is,*
> *and all fullness of his nature, without also knowing God.*
>
> —T. T. MUNGER

A MIRACLE

In 1994 I was taking large amounts of prednisone and five other drugs to control eosinophilic gastroenteritis (EGE), which had flared up again. According to the specialists I'd seen, I would now need to take the medications for the rest of my life. Although these medicines had potentially harmful and life-shortening side effects, I accepted the risks because they gave me relief from my debilitating symptoms.

In March, Ken and I attended an alternative medical conference in San Diego. Though very ill, I completed intense interviews with three prominent physicians, including one with Larry Dossey, MD, about his book *Healing Words: The Power of Prayer in Medicine*. In preparation for the interview, I had read five of his other books, as well as current articles about the effect of faith on healing.

By the time we boarded our plane for home, I was exhausted. I earnestly desired the kind of healing Dr. Dossey talked about in his work, and as I reclined in my airplane seat, I prayed, *Father, if it is Your will for me, I ask that You heal me.* Although I struggled with doubt, I continued to pray until sleep overtook me.

About two hours later, a distinct physical sensation startled me awake. I felt a gaggle of goose bumps start at my feet and spread rapidly over my entire body. After a few seconds, the bumps mysteriously disappeared. I didn't hear heavenly voices, no bright lights flashed, and my appearance didn't change. But somehow I felt *different.*

Some time later, still unsure of what had occurred, I turned to Ken and said, "I know this may sound odd, but I believe I have just been healed."

He gazed at me and said nothing.

"Honey," I said, "I'm going to stop all my medications. I really believe that my body is healed. What do you think about that?"

Ken was silent for a moment, and I couldn't tell what he was thinking. It was years before I learned that my words had terrified him.

At the time, all he said was: "Shelley, knowing you, I doubt there would be much I could say or do to change your mind. Just promise me two things. First, check it out with your internal medicine and allergy specialists. Next, if you have any symptoms after you stop the medications, please be willing to restart them immediately. You know how risky it is to stop taking prednisone abruptly."

I squeezed his hand and promised. Three days later, I consulted with my two specialists and stopped all medications. Now, several years later, I am still free from the symptoms of EGE.

Through this healing, I came to a much deeper understanding of the connection between my mind, body, and spirit and how important it is to know the God who created them and to have a relationship with Him.

In order to be a realist you must believe in miracles.

— HENRY CHRISTOPHER BAILEY

BECAUSE HE LOVES US

Being right with God enables us to be right with others. It strengthens our resolve to discover what authority truly guides right living. God's love is not alien, imposed from without. It is woven into the very fabric of our being.

Because God loves us, He has programmed us to distinguish right from wrong. His yes and His no echo from deep within us. Yet we are also born with an inclination to transgress. And because He loves us—and desires a genuine love from us in return—God allows us to choose to follow Him or to go our own way.

When I choose to stay close to God, my understanding of and compassion for others increase, and I experience a growing sense of inner peace, even when caught in the midst of life's storms. I now realize that in learning life's lessons, I do not stand alone. Knowing God is what enables us to clear the hurdles and stay on track. It is what renews our willingness to face and learn from life's challenges. It is what restores our joy by enabling us to love ourselves and others.

Because we love Him

Knowledge avails us nothing if we don't put into practice what we know. The same is true of our knowledge of God. HIRTL and TRACK are two metaphors for the life-enhancing concepts that help us do just that. HIRTL is a metaphor to help us know love; TRACK is a metaphor to help us know God. To know God is to know love on the superhuman level. The more mindful we are of staying on track to knowing Him, the more likely we are to clear the hurdles and know love on the human level.

We are human and we will get off track. What happens when we do? When runners get off track because of an injury, fatigue, or stepping out of bounds, they decide what they need to do before they return to the track for the next event. We do the same. When we get off track, we do not throw up our hands and quit. Instead, we view the setback as a challenge. We learn from our failure and then rest and heal by caring for our minds, bodies, and spirits. Then we resume training. We return to the race.

> *Knowledge, if it does not determine action, is dead to us.*
>
> —PLOTINUS

The life-enhancing concepts that will help you clear the hurdles and stay on track are as close as your fingertips. Starting with the little fingers, put your fingers together one by one. This simple exercise will remind you that:

Honesty comes when we admit the *Truth.*
Integrity comes when we take *Responsibility.*
Respect comes when we maintain a great *Attitude.*
Trust comes when we develop *Character.*
Love comes when we act on our *Knowledge* of God.

And remember—all of this starts with our thoughts. We reap in our lives what we sow in our minds. In *The Sampler* I have shared with you what I reaped when I sowed negative thoughts in my own life. In His great grace, forgiveness, and love, God transformed my mind—and that has transformed my life. What I am in the process of becoming is my gift to Him.

I begin and end each day's devotion with the Lord's Prayer and the prayer of St. Francis of Assisi. For me, they represent the essence of right living. They help me to clear the hurdles and stay on track. Wishing you God's blessings, I leave with you the prayer of St. Francis:

Lord, make me an instrument of your peace.
Where there is hatred, let me sow love;
Where there is injury, pardon;
Where there is doubt, faith;
Where there is despair, hope;
Where there is darkness, light;
Where there is sadness, joy;
O divine Master, grant that I may not so much seek
to be consoled as to console,
to be understood as to understand,
to be loved as to love.

For it is in giving that we receive;
it is in pardoning that we are pardoned;
and it is in dying that we are born to eternal life.
Amen

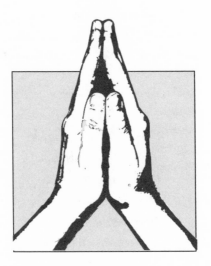

Epilogue

Seated here at my desk finishing up my thoughts to you,
I look up to see the wonderful sampler my mother left to
me. I pray the message will inspire you on your journey,
as it continues to inspire me:

> What we are is
> God's gift to us
> What we become is
> our gift to God

Thank You

To Clay Starlin, for your sensitivity and skill in clarifying my thoughts while keeping my words and voice intact. Without God's grace and your collaboration, *The Sampler* would never have been started.

To Judith St. Pierre, for your God-given gifts of editing and teaching, which helped my message flow from my heart to the page. Without God's love and your guidance, *The Sampler* would never have been finished.

To my family: my husband, Ken, for your loving partnership and constructive critiques throughout the writing process; my late father, Lawrence Maurice, for teaching me the importance of a disciplined work ethic and an organized environment; my brother, Michael Maurice, for your steadfast loyalty and constant love; Aunt Fanchon Blake, for your inspiration and special stories; and Aunt Jean Gesford, for our many long and loving discussions on accepting what is.

To all who read *The Sampler,* suggested ways to improve it, and encouraged me to keep writing: Carol

Abraham, Susan Ashton, Karen Balkwill, Cindy Clague, Rick Cleveland, Cary English, Sharon Goodmonson, Ethlyn and William Luce, Diane Mattoon, Barbara McKee, Debbie Newman, Mike Quillin, Lee Roberts, Ann Salvaladena, Ronni Sullivan, and Vicki Wilson.

And to all my wonderful friends, family, and clients, who continue to teach me about love and life.

About the Author

Since 1983, Shelley Maurice-Maier has practiced as a licensed physician's assistant in family medicine, with special interests in women's health, chronic illness, pain control, grief counseling, anxiety, and depression. Since a miraculous healing in 1994, she has devoted her practice entirely to mind-health counseling. In that year she received training and board certification in Eriksonian mental health counseling, and subsequently the Oregon Board of Medical Examiners granted her an extended medical practice description as an insight behavioral psychotherapist.

In 1994, Shelley established The Heart of Health, a nonprofit corporation that produced a weekly television series promoting mind-body medicine. Topics included discussions of the effectiveness of prayer, acupuncture, guided imagery, relaxation response, homeopathy, biofeedback, and nutritional impact on patient health. In the first series, Shelley interviewed Oregon physicians and psychologists whose methods combined traditional Western medicine with alternative therapies. In the second series, she interviewed internationally recognized authorities in medicine, psychology, and science. Her guests included Bernie Siegel, MD, Larry Dossey, MD, David T. Riley, MD, Lawrence Le Shan, PhD, and Jean Achtenberg, PhD.

You can contact Shelley at
www.shelleymauricemaier.com.

ABIDING BOOKS

Are you dreaming of turning your God-honoring message into a high-quality, marketable book? We can help.

Abiding Books is a network of Christian professionals dedicated to providing the editing, design, production, and promotion services you need to see your dream come true. From getting your ideas down on paper to getting your books into stores, we give you all the help you need.

· EDITING, COPYEDITING, AND PROOFREADING

· COVER DESIGN

· MANUSCRIPT REVIEWING AND CRITIQUING

· STYLES SETTING

· INTERIOR DESIGN AND TYPESETTING

· MARKETING AND PUBLICITY

· PRINT BUYING

· PROMOTIONAL WRITING

· REPACKS AND REVISIONS

Of all the writers who try to get their manuscript published by a royalty publisher, less than 1 percent succeed. That's why more and more authors are turning to publishing alternatives. Your message is important to us. We will give it the attention it deserves and help you turn it into a book that will read, look, and sell just like books produced by the top royalty publishers.

E-mail us at: info@abidingbooks.com

An Abiding Book not only looks good—it is good!